Earth Roots Sing
Ellie Ann Deighton

Copyright © 2025 by Ellie Ann Deighton

All rights reserved.

No part of this publication may be reproduced, distributed, or transmitted in any form or by any means, including photocopying, recording, or other electronic or mechanical methods, without the prior written permission of the publisher, except as permitted by Australian copyright law. For permission requests or bulk orders, contact the author.

The story, all names, characters, and incidents portrayed in this production are fictitious. No identification with actual persons (living or deceased), places, buildings, and products is intended or should be inferred.

Book Cover by Ellie Ann Deighton

1st Edition 2025

Contents

Epigraph	1
Ellie's Earth	2
Dedication	4
Foreword	7
1. Voices	11
2. Missions	51
3. Community	63
4. Songs	83
Your Everlasting Symphony	133
'It' is GOLD	137
About the author	139
Author's note	141
Permission To Pivot	143
Acknowledgements	145

Your voice is powerful.

When you weave your voice openly, expressively and freely you will grow roots that are healthy, real and beautiful.

Your true voice brings connection.

When you silence your voice, hide your voice, pretend your voice is something that it isn't, you rob yourself of who you truly are.

This poisons the roots.

~ evidence suggests

ELLIE'S EARTH ROOTS

FICTION
Ankhara Codes I: An Adventure to Essence
Ankhara Codes II: Allies of the Soul
Ankhara Codes III: A Devotion To Peace

ORACLE CARDS
Fruits of the Feminine

POETRY
'It' is GOLD
Fire Body Warm
Silver Witch Rose
Water River Run
Air Breathes Light
Salt Sugar Spirit

NON-FICTION
Myths of a Mystic Woman
Dreams of the Wild Soul

MUSIC ALBUMS
Temple Calling: An Album For Your Altar

ONLINE TRAININGS & COURSES:
The Wild Soul Mastery

more at elliedeighton.com

This is the seventh book of seven in The Elemental Collection; a poetry series focused on the seven essential elements of fulfilment.

You can read The Elemental Collection in any order you choose.

EARTH ROOTS SING

For Peggy,
Who could sing as beautifully as her birds,
For Daphne,
Who wasn't a singer but wow, she could speak.
My grandmothers,
Who are now in their gardens in the sky
And who are the reasons I can sing down here on Earth.
And finally, for you,
Reading these words and singing with me.

ELLIE ANN DEIGHTON

Foreword

In my journal I wrote...

July 15 2025

End result: To meet my muse and be informed of the calling of my heart; Earth Roots Sing.

I am the magic
And the muse
And I am here
To say to you:

That you came here to sing
Finally here on Earth
You came here to be yourself
That's why your mother gave birth
You came here to be a star
To shine in your own way
You came here to walk your path
So listen when I say

Your voice holds a pattern
It's a pattern from the stars
Perhaps a pattern from Venus
Perhaps a pattern from Mars
But a pattern nonetheless
And a magic has come through
Right through your body
You don't have to know what to do
You just have to know to sing
To let your voice echo out
And know it can be softly
You don't have to scream and shout
For a voice that is true
Will slice through the silence
And cut through noise too
Offering an inner guidance
So when you're feeling lost
You can take a breath and sing
When you're covered in frost
Your voice can lift the freeze
When you feel like running
Your voice can set you free
Like a story of becoming
Your voice begins to lead
I sing through my body
When life is feeling stuck
I sing for everybody
When the group is feeling yuck

But really the song is for myself
It's who we truly are
Our voices unleashed, real as seashells
A magic that starts a spark
A fleck of dirt that soon uplifts
And smudges across your shirt
To remind you, you are part of this
It's natural to be covered in earth
So it doesn't matter
If your voice breaks
And everything falls apart
You will not shatter
If your voice shakes
It's okay to reveal your heart
So reveal your chest
Open your song
And let the rhythm of you out
You are blessed
Hiding times are gone
The harmony will sing itself out
For when you sing the patterns of the stars
Your roots will lock in deeper
You'll be connected to all your parts
Your consciousness expands, it's no secret
It's just what happens when you sing yourself
When your voice comes, your words for the taking
You anchor in your body, bring glory to your health
When your voice comes, your silence is forsaken

Now that doesn't mean there's no time to reflect
It simply means your voice is online
Your wounding can rise, you can feel a reject
And more singing will heal you over time
It's all a facade, this need now to hush
To quiet yourself so as not to be cancelled
So take off the mask, pull your feet from the mud
And be wild, this is you, shackles dismantled.

Welcome to Earth.

Voices
the patterns of the stars

It isn't meant to be silent
The voice that is calling to you
The voice that begs to speak through you
It is loud
If you listen down to the root of it
Because
Earth roots sing
They have a harmony to them
And it doesn't matter if it is a harmony you have heard before
If it is familiar, like an old friend
Or new, like someone you are excited to meet
It matters that it is your voice
And you can hear it
– You are a singer on the inside

EARTH ROOTS SING

On the inside you are a singer

There is a song that moves you

A reason you love certain types of music

A reason songs make you dance

There is a rhythm inside you

A beating of a drum

A strumming of a guitar

The keys of a piano laced across your insides

It's all there

Inside you

Your body is the instrument

It's okay if you don't define yourself as 'musical'

It's not strictly about music

It's the way you run in time

It's the way you speak to an audience

It's the way you write poetry

It's the way you make love

It's the way you feel without filter

It's the kindness you offer

It's the power you refuse to waiver in

It's the friendship you share

It's the softness in you

It's the fierceness in you

All these parts

All these different bars of your song

And you are the singer

The lead performer
The main character
The central voice
– You might not be acting like the lead singer but you're it

EARTH ROOTS SING

You are also the drummer
Keeping to the beat
Creating the undertone
Setting the stage for the performance
And you are on the keys
Decorating the rhythm with beauty
And the lead guitarist
Offering flare after flare
You are the whole band
Just as your whole body is a part of nature
– You just might not have put the band together yet

There's this thing here on Earth in business
That we must niche
That we must pick one thing
Spend ten thousand hours with it
Master it
And let that be our thing
You know the saying
Jack of all trades and master of none
Alluding to our single ability to master one skill
Or we've spread ourselves too thin and it's over now
Well
Let me tell you how to bust that myth
Be yourself
For real
Notice the different things that call to you and be all in with them
Do not tippy toe
I am a writer so I write often
I am a singer so I sing often
I am a teacher so I teach often

I am a coach so I coach often
I am a witch so I witch often
I am a wife so I wife often
I am fit so I do fitness often
I am a daughter so I daughter often
You know?
I put the energy in across the board
And is it true that I write less books because of all the other stuff?
Sure! Maybe!
But I'm also more fulfilled
And the music informs the storytelling and uplifts my relationships
And the relationships uplift my witchcraft and inform my rituals
And the rituals uplift my fitness and inform my marriage
And it's all connected
So I call bullshit
I am no 'jack of all trades'
I am simply my entire earthly existence
– Let yourself sing all your songs

The way I sing my songs
Helps everything in my life dance
And I really do sing
But maybe you build
Maybe you are an excellent sportsperson
Perhaps you are a world-class teacher
The most incredible driver
A loving parent
A star
You didn't come to Earth to be a 'part' of yourself
You came here to be you
– Being yourself is a beautiful song

EARTH ROOTS SING

At the end of the day
And in the beginning
There is just you and your voice
And everything in between
Is you deciding
Will you let your voice be heard?
Will you let yourself be loud?
Will you be so bold as to sing the truth?
– Be bold, singer

ELLIE ANN DEIGHTON

There are those who sing loudly
Take up centre stage
Have no qualms about being the noisy one
In fact they detest the quiet
They fear being forgotten
So they compensate with their noise
They practice practice practice
They'll sing in front of anyone
They've become quite the performer
But they're forgetting the most important part of the performance
It's the feeling
The realness
The authentic offering of the heart
And they are loud and it is awesome
So should they be themselves
Absolutely yes should they have this confidence
But they are feigning a bigger insecurity

EARTH ROOTS SING

They actually fear their voices
The ones that come out when the earth roots rise
Because the earth roots bring emotion
They are connected to everything
They bypass nothing
They share the truth
They reveal the essence
And that is the scariest voice to reveal
For that is the most vulnerable voice to be rejected
But a funny thing happens
When the loud one lets the earth roots rise
It's like a superpower
Their vulnerability becomes a sacred weapon
And before they know it
They are sharing their voice unbound
No fucks given for the performance
All fucks given to the moment
– Let your earth roots rise

There are those who sing loudly
And it may bother you
It may throw you off
They may not even be as brilliant as you
They may be quite good, but not quite in their genius
And it's your genius to be loud
It's your truth to be on stage
But you're not
And they are
And you see it's less about talent
Less about how good you are
More about putting yourself in the ring
More about being willing to reveal yourself and play the game
It's about letting yourself be the star that you are
– Get on stage, singer

EARTH ROOTS SING

You might not be a singer,
But you do have a true stage
The music thing can be literal
But it can be symbolic!
You can be a star in any field
You can be on stage as yourself
You can sing, sing, sing phenomenal harmonies
As an engineer
As a dentist
As a surgeon
As a nurse
As a funeral director
I mean, wow, these people can sing
I've never seen a team so poetic as those at the funeral parlour
They way they speak
The grace they hold you in
The patience they have
Everything is urgent and there is truly limited time but to them...
Nothing is in a hurry
Everything is okay
Their support is the ever-present beating of a drum
Through one of the most challenging rites of passage in our modern world today
Death
And in the pillar of death they stand
They sing for life
For the life that was
And the life that still is

And the life to come
And they let you grieve
They care not to block or stop your tears
It is all allowed
And you are encouraged in your own way
To share your voice with your one now in spirit
Maybe you'll write a note to slip in the coffin
Maybe you'll speak
Maybe you'll telepathically say secret words during the reflections
Maybe you'll sing
Maybe you'll toast
Maybe you'll cry
But you'll do you
You will find it in you to rise above the fear of public speaking
Because in the moment
Everything falls away except for you and that one person
It's just between you and their spirit now
And you'll know exactly what is yours to do
And the funeral team will let you dance
– Everyone is a singer

At my grandfather's funeral I knew
It wasn't for me to speak
It wasn't my truth
I helped Nan write the eulogy
I sat back
I cried in the pews
I offered an unreleased recording of my song Rebel Rose
Tweaked a little
Because he didn't have a womb
But he was a rebel
And he was a rose
The most romantic of hearts
Under the most intense bush of thorns
But this time
In my grandmother's passing
I knew
Immediately
It was for me to speak
It was for me to sing live, not pre-recorded
It was for me to be involved
It was for me to come, not because I was in support of Nan at all the meetings
But because I was in support of the true voice of the service
I was in devotion to Nan's voice being the voice on the day that was heard
I wrote my speech
And cried and cried and cried
It is a healing thing to be in your voice

Which we'll circle back to later
But I wrote my speech
And I read it to my mother
Worried I wouldn't get through it
But I did
And I looked at her after as she sat there in silence
Asked her, 'What do you think?'
She looked at me
I felt like she'd stripped me back to my soul
Like somehow she had completely revealed all of me
My gosh I felt naked
Like I had revealed the secrets of how I really felt about her
My mother's mother
Poked a hole in my mother's grief with the wand of my words
And she said,
'You have captured her perfectly.'
Because that was exactly her
The spirit I had captured
In the moment of writing this
Tomorrow is the day I will get on that stage and speak it
And let me tell you
I am afraid
Because there is nothing quite like sharing the true voice that lives within us
To reveal that voice
To open that voice
To share that voice
Oh there is nothing quite like it

EARTH ROOTS SING

But tomorrow
I will rise to speak
I will share my voice
And Nan will be the only person I'll be speaking to
And that's how you get through it
You speak to who you are meant to speak to
You delete the rest from the audience of your mind
And you offer your heart
– Earth roots sing to the people they are meant for

If you write a book
There will be people who cherish those words as their new bible
Who reference the pages like a tarot deck
Who receive the wisdom like an oracle
And there will be people who do not care
Who think, 'Good for you' and move on, never to think of your book ever again
There will be people who read it and hate it
Who take it apart and decide it's better used as toilet paper
Or perhaps fuel to a flame
And they will burn it
They might even use their voices to tell you about it
But the trick
Is to focus on your people
And write the most unfiltered offering you can
Because the people your voice is singing to will be changed
And that's how the world rises up
– We sing to each other

EARTH ROOTS SING

Have you ever seen someone sing
Heard their voice
And wished for it?
Wished for that tone?
Wished for that melodic magic?
The trick is not to wish for their voice
The trick is to find yours
– When you find your voice you'll never wish for anyone else's

There are many in the world
Who have silenced themselves
And they may say
'My mother silenced me'
'My father silenced me'
'My religion silenced me'
'My world silenced me'
But *they* silenced *themselves*
They made the choice not to speak
And I am not saying it doesn't suck
Or that there aren't places in the world where sharing your voice is harder than others
But I am saying
That all throughout history
That all throughout the world
Magic has happened when people sing
And even if you aren't to be the next biggest hit
You have a voice
You have a spirit that can sing
And so do they
And they can root down into it
– Deeper roots help in harder times

There are hard times
There are places where your voice may not be heard
For example
There are countries where I cannot touch my wife
Without risk of imprisonment
Or worse
Isn't it wild?
That love can be so offensive
But that is the pain of a world full of people who aren't in their voice
A world full of suppressed sexual energy
Don't let them cum, but give them a gun
And see what happens?
Bury them in shame, without speaking, perhaps some screaming
And see what happens?
The world is hurting
But nothing is more hurtful for a person than losing their voice
For the voice is the microphone of the soul
– Earth roots cry

ELLIE ANN DEIGHTON

If the voice is the microphone of the soul
Imagine turning that off!
– Earth ro~~ots~~ *madness*

If the voice is the microphone of the soul
Imagine turning that on!
– Earth roots glowing

ELLIE ANN DEIGHTON

If the voice is the microphone of the soul
Imagine steadying the hum
– Earth roots smiling

There are others who will walk up to the switch
To the on-off switch of your soul microphone
And they will flick it if you let them
Sometimes it's brilliant
Like the magic of a friend who will go to battle for you
Ensuring that switch is flicked on every damn day
And they're still kind, these friends,
They'll let you have a day off
They'll let you switch off and cry
But then, 'Back on!' they will shout
They will encourage
They will snap you back out of it
'It' being the slump of the off switch
And it's not because they don't accept you in your pain
It's because they know your heart
They see your greatness
And they see your voice
And they want you to shine
There are teachers like this
There are parents like this
There are siblings like this
There are strangers like this
And there are people who are so far lost
They have so long forgotten what it's like to have their switch on
That they are screaming into the void
Determined to take your light with them
They will stop at nothing to flick off your switch
They will convince you it is the best course of action

They will tell you that you suck when it's on
They'll convince you the switch on is cringey
They'll cancel you with all their might
And the power move you have in your pocket at all times
Not against these people
Not even for them
But for yourself
Is that you can leave on your switch
For the light of your voice
For the magic of your voice
For the roots of your voice
Are what make your soul untouchable
– Soul voice ON

They say, 'Let the haters hate'
Which could be irresponsible
Or could be true
But what if, instead of focusing on the haters
You focused on your switch
– Turn the switch of your soul's microphone on and see what happens

ELLIE ANN DEIGHTON

When there is indecision?
– Turn on the soul's microphone

When there is conflict?
– Turn on the soul's microphone

ELLIE ANN DEIGHTON

When there is a lot at stake?
– Turn on the soul's microphone

When it appears all is lost?
– Turn on the soul's microphone

When there's nothing left to do?
– Turn on the soul's microphone

When you're down and out and convinced you're broken?
– Turn on the soul's microphone

ELLIE ANN DEIGHTON

When you are rising into a new momentum?
– Turn up the soul's microphone

EARTH ROOTS SING

When you feel like you're finally getting it?
– Turn up the soul's microphone

ELLIE ANN DEIGHTON

When your friend is struggling and you still hear their truth?
– Turn up their soul's microphone

When your beloved has an empty cup?
– Turn up your soul's microphone and while you're at it, turn up the volume on theirs

When all else fails?
– Turn up the microphone of your soul and speak

Truth reveals itself when you talk
Because the truth has a ring to it
Ever say something to a friend and realise it isn't true?
And because you are in your bubble with them you explore it?
Hang on... that isn't true, it's more like...
And then in bouncing your words off them you figure it out
Or because they know your real voice they'll reflect it back to you
That's how easy it can be to come to truth
That's how available it is to come to truth
– Such is the power of the voice

ELLIE ANN DEIGHTON

I'm not saying talk at everyone and talk nonstop
I'm saying speak with intention and see what happens
– Earth roots reveal

Missions
the eagerness in our bones

ELLIE ANN DEIGHTON

Right underneath
All the weight others have placed on you
All the pain you have received
All the memories projected onto to you
All the versions of you that you've been
There's a real you
Underneath all of that
Having grown through all of that
But essentially unchanged
And the real you?
The real you knows your mission
– Earth roots here on purpose

EARTH ROOTS SING

You know your mission
And it amazes me how you pretend you don't
How many people pretend they don't
And it's not your fault
It's not their fault
It's the fault of a way of a people who have become like sheep
Chosen to fit in over standing out
Because we should all stand out
It's part of what makes us properly fit in
Authentically fit in
Authentically fitting in is a very different game
It's a game where each of us is a puzzle piece
And each of us is a slightly different shape
And we all fit together
We complement each other
And if you have lost sight of your mission
You're in the right place
And if you have full sight of your mission
You're in the right place
– Earth roots fit together

There is a mission in your bones
A bigger reason you are here
A grander picture
A real calling
And if you don't know what it is
I invite you to wonder
If this were your last day on Earth
What would you talk about to your loved ones?
For example
My late grandmother spent time with us before she passed and she said,
'Make your art'
'Be respectful of others, but most importantly respect yourself'
'Do what you want to do with your life, regardless of whether other people understand it'
'Just live a wonderful life and look out for each other'
And you can tell by reading her words what she valued
You can even tell she was an artist
And a teacher
And she cared for her family and friends more than anything else
But she was also kind to strangers
And she wasn't worried about other people's opinions
Though she was eager to learn
And she really cared for her own opinion
She wasn't perfect
As none of us are
But she had her ways
And she lived her mission

And she knew when it was over
She was at peace with that
That's why she could articulate so clearly
So I invite you to imagine
Imagine it's about to be over!
And I hope for you it is not
But who knows
Maybe you're ninety-one and ready like my grandmother was
Maybe not
But your mission is there
It's right underneath the topsoil
And you can know it so intimately
Just imagine you can
Start to talk about it to a friend
Start to write about it in your journal
Because once you identify your mission
You can double down
– Earth roots live their mission if you let them

ELLIE ANN DEIGHTON

When you double down on your mission

Lend your voice to your purpose

Open your heart in the direction you are called

Doors open

Hearts flower

Friendships blossom

Love deepens

Memories are made

The pathway reveals itself

And you will find fulfilment

And you will take risks

Because the greatest risk is to lose your mission

And the greatest gain is to live it

And suddenly you'll be able to support other people's mission

Because the thread of a core soul mission is recognisable

There are missions we are familiar with

A certain Aussie croc-lover with a wildlife mission,

A certain king of times past with a mission to create the United Kingdom,

Missions aren't just in famous people,

They're just in people

And you have one too

– Have you sat with your earthly mission yet?

My earthly mission is one of articulation
I can communicate an unseen frequency
Support it in being felt
Translate it to someone who doesn't speak that language
Put it in a song
Tell it in story form
Teach it in a course so others can do the same
I'm an articulate renaissance woman
And when I realised offering transmissions in different forms was my gift
Suddenly I didn't feel like a jack of all trades
It made sense that I was a singer, writer, coach, speaker, teacher, sportswoman,
Because yes of course I can have it all
Of course I can communicate in different ways
So if you like me are a multifaceted creative
A multi-talented person
I invite you to look and ask
What's the common branch?
Mine is communication and empowerment
Uplifting, emotive, inspirational
And yes it's different if I'm writing or singing,
But the branches are common
The leaves are leaning on each other
And the further I climb out on the branch, the wider I spread my wings
Be yourself
Notice the branches

And climb out

So the roots can grow deep

– Earth roots connect

If I could have any superpower
I would want to know all forms of language
ALL
Take me to an ancient cave?
I can read it.
Introduce me to an alien species?
I got this.
Drop me off in a foreign country?
I'll find my way.
Introduce me to a lost traveller?
I'll help them.
Want to watch a non-English movie?
I'd love to.
– Earth roots are the superpower I already have

ELLIE ANN DEIGHTON

Earth roots are a superpower
They dig you into the earth
Anchor you into your human experience
In a world that is so technological
So out of body
So catered towards escapism
Your earth roots pull you in
Plug you into your power in your body
Remind you who you were born to be
Keep you connected to your mission
And when you really find them
When you allow them to flourish
Your earth roots will help you to sing
– Sink into your earth roots

So how do you make your earth roots flourish?

Step one: Find your roots

Step two: Love your roots

Step three: Find your people who love your roots

Step four: REPEAT

– Your earth roots make everything easy because their mission is for you to be you

ELLIE ANN DEIGHTON

Community
right there cheerleading us

Trees have friends
They talk to each other
Science says
Spirit says
We can all feel it if we try
And we all know we feel better with a little bit more foot-planting on the earth
A little bit more time spent with feet on the grass
A little bit more time spent immersed in nature
A few days in the wild and we unwind and relax
And yeah, we are a bit far removed
Some of us struggle with the bugs and spiders
The creepy crawlies
We aren't familiar with our own backyards
And again, it's not our fault we were raised this way
It's not our parent's fault either
It just is the way it is
But it's our choice to do something different
To let the trees be our people again
And to be with the people who let our nature sing
And I think that's the point
More nature, more you, more songs, more magic
That's what you were born for
That's what you are here walking towards
Right?
– Earth roots say so

Finish this sentence:
My people are...
– Earth roots say you already know

My people are interested in bettering themselves
Not because they are inherently broken
But because they have a zest for life
They want to live a wonderful life
They believe in magic
They live in a world where magic is real
Connected to the earth
Inspired by nature's creatures
Including themselves
Including me
Including their families
Including their wider communities
They are agents of connection
Not bothered by agents of separation
Because they know their path
They're on their mission
And a person on a mission isn't swayed by someone else's
– Earth roots know each other

EARTH ROOTS SING

When you know your mission
Someone else won't sway you
Inspire you?
Absolutely
Teach you?
For sure
Show you how not to go about the mission?
Haha abso-fucking-lutely
But they will not sway you.
They may catch your attention for a moment
Distract you for a while
But the deeper into your mission you travel
The harder to pull you away
And the more you know yourself
The more awake you'll stay
– Earth roots are focused

The more you connect to the roots of who you are

Your earth roots

The more you will notice

That there are people who bring you closer to the root

People who try to pull the roots out

Replace them with their own roots

But the replacement roots aren't real

They are an illusion

A made up stick of connective tissue

They don't offer you anything

They certainly don't serve you

And it's important to notice

When you spend time with a person:

Are you more rooted in who you are?

Have they uprooted you?

Have you let them replace your roots?

Have you let them trim your roots?

Have your roots retracted back into your body?

A question I ask my clients is:

Are your feet in your feet?

And sometimes they say

No, my feet are in my chest

And so I tell them

Take a moment

Close your eyes

Connect to yourself

Let the breath in your body bring your feet down

Take your time

EARTH ROOTS SING

And when you're back in yourself let me know
We'll go from there
Because I'm not here to create people
I'm not there to fill them up with me
I'm there to support them being rooted in themselves
Changing into whoever they were born to be
Shedding any version of themselves they thought they had to become
So they can be their earth roots
And finally
When they are rooted into themselves so deeply
They can open their mouths
Share their missions
And sing
– Earth roots sing in my body and yours

I wrote a song about the earth roots
Funnily enough
I wrote it in the forest
Sitting on the earth
Surrounded by beautiful people
With a guitar I borrowed from my sister
On a rug I borrowed from my mum
Sleeping in a swag I borrowed from my friends
At a gathering I was invited to by a client
And there's no way you'll ever convince me that we aren't all connected
 – Earth roots bring us home to each other and through each other

I used to struggle to ask for support

And if I imagine

Connect

Look through my mind's eye

At the way my roots were then

I see little roots

Tiny shoots

Trying really hard to stick in the ground and flourish

But I kept pulling them up

Because every time I was guided towards support

I panicked

I uprooted myself

I ran

And started again

New, tiny shoots

Just into the ground

Intimacy that would tear me up and have me rip them out

And start again

New, tiny shoots

Just into the ground

Vulnerability that was or wasn't accepted and I wouldn't find out

I'd harvest myself prematurely

And start again

Until I'd decide

To plant them in

And let them stick

And know I could still travel and move and dance and spread my wings

And be rooted in love

Be grounded in service
Be connected in my relationships
Be supported by the ones I love
Be met beautifully by new strangers
And when I use my mind's eye now
To see the roots of me
They are strong
Growing
Winding down
Wrapping around others as if in a dance
Met in a mutual twist
And it's a beautiful vision
There's plenty of space for growth
But I don't have to go anywhere
I can ask for help
I can be attacked and it doesn't hit me
I am whole, connected to my roots
I can feel myself all the time no matter who I'm with
The roots are bare and wild and free
And I have the sense that is how I am meant to be
– And so I am the earth roots

EARTH ROOTS SING

I would rather
Fewer friends
Than 'friends' who will only have me with a certain type of root
– Earth roots accept

ELLIE ANN DEIGHTON

I would rather
My friends challenge me
Than feel like they can't deepen their roots
– Earth roots grow together

EARTH ROOTS SING

I would rather

Live my mission

Than shrivel in the facade of service to another

– Earth roots challenge me to be me

ELLIE ANN DEIGHTON

I would rather
Eat cake and love it
Than torture myself with a parsnip
But you can eat what you want
– Earth roots aren't here to judge

EARTH ROOTS SING

I loved myself
When I was severely overweight
So much so that they didn't see it
My friends didn't think of me as fit
But they didn't think of me as fat either
They would say as I transformed,
"Wow, you look so thin and toned,
But what were you before?"
– I would say I'd forgotten my earth roots

There are side effects
I don't want to scare you
But there are side effects
Of disconnection from the earth
The kind of side effects you don't want to think about
And I won't go into detail
But you can already see the imbalance
You already know what happens to you
Because it is a personal thing
Our relationship to the earth
And the way we feel the pain when we lose part of it
– Earth roots are healthy, naturally

When I wanted to lose weight
It was less about the fat
More about the truth
That I knew this wasn't my picture of health
And my people loved me for who I was
Accepted me wherever I was
That's a key, by the way
A beautiful thing
But it's also great to be able to share the adventure of coming home to yourself
To say, 'Alright guys, time to move my body in a new way'
And to be received in celebration
To be encouraged
Without being shamed
I have lost weight
And eaten treats
I have gained weight
And starved myself
And the way I have learnt
Is to be connected to my body as the earth
And to ask myself what she needs
And to respect her as I would a tree
Let myself be in my seasons and let myself have my friends and let myself be seen
And know that all of it is nature
The ebbs and the flows
And my people are there in spirit with me the whole time
– Earth roots are a journey

ELLIE ANN DEIGHTON

Draw a tree
– Earth roots dare you

EARTH ROOTS SING

You inspire each other
When you have real friends
You'll have different gifts
And some that are similar
And you'll trigger each other
If you're really friends and you really spend time and you are real in that time
You will trigger each other
Because that's what happens when you connect
You see more of one another
And more isn't always better
It can be flawed
It can be embarrassing
It can be hilarious
It can be brilliant
It won't always be a certain way
It will always be more if you let it
And if you do
And you are blessed to trigger each other
And you take the opportunity to walk into that fire
Step through the window to the soul
Rise above the heaviness that threatens to drag you down
Wow
You will know each other as you do yourself
Eventually
And you will learn
It's okay to be you
– Earth roots heal

ELLIE ANN DEIGHTON

Songs
passed through all of time and space

ELLIE ANN DEIGHTON

Earth hums
She is present underfoot
A tone we lay upon
A frequency we dance to
Earth is where we return
Over and over and over in our lives
And of course, in the end
Earth is where we go
Where the dust goes and settles
Where the ashes go and rest
But what never ends
Is her song
And the way her roots reach down
Touching every one of us along the way
– Earth roots sing

EARTH ROOTS SING

Earth roots sing
To my heart
Tell me I'm shining
When I don't know where to start
Take my hand
And pull me through
I don't need to know yet
What to do
Earth roots sing
To my mind
Tell me I'm shining
One of a kind
Take my feet
Guide me home
All your messages
Remind me how far I've come
Earth roots sing
To my body
Tell me I remember
To be honest
Take my soul
And light the way
There's no such thing
As being guided astray
Earth roots sing to you
All the puzzle pieces are inside you too
Take my spirit
We are one

ELLIE ANN DEIGHTON

There's no way I'll be silent
Let's sing our songs
To the earth
Where we stand
To the earth
Because she sings back
– The *Earth Roots Sing* song

EARTH ROOTS SING

She sings back
The earth, that is
When we listen to her
And when we don't
In my hardest times
I have leant on a tree
And I have listened
I have sat on a stone
And I have listened
I have stared at a snake
And I have listened
And always
Without fail
She has sung to me
– The earth's roots sing

ELLIE ANN DEIGHTON

When I feel my roots are shrivelled
– The earth still sings

EARTH ROOTS SING

When I feel my roots have deepened
– The earth still sings

ELLIE ANN DEIGHTON

When I feel I have grown to be the tallest tree
– The earth still sings

When I am taking up a lot of space
– The earth still sings

ELLIE ANN DEIGHTON

When I am hiding
– The earth still sings

EARTH ROOTS SING

When I am thriving
– The earth still sings

ELLIE ANN DEIGHTON

When I am dying
– The earth still sings

EARTH ROOTS SING

When I am alone
– The earth still sings

ELLIE ANN DEIGHTON

When I am surrounded
– The earth still sings

EARTH ROOTS SING

When I am on my mission
– The earth still sings

When I forget my mission
– The earth still sings

EARTH ROOTS SING

When I have incredible friends
– The earth still sings

ELLIE ANN DEIGHTON

When I have been an arsehat
– The earth still sings

When I have failed
– The earth still sings

ELLIE ANN DEIGHTON

When I am overseas
– The earth still sings

EARTH ROOTS SING

When I am married
– The earth still sings

ELLIE ANN DEIGHTON

When I am depleted
– The earth still sings

EARTH ROOTS SING

When I am nourished
– The earth still sings

ELLIE ANN DEIGHTON

When I am anything
The earth still sings
So I might as well be myself
And sing my own song in response
– The earth and I sing best together

EARTH ROOTS SING

When I first began to harmonise
I would do so with myself
Those were the days of iPods
So yes, kids,
A separate device for music
It didn't all fit on our phones
I'd voice record in the iPod,
Loop it through a speaker and voice record with a phone,
Then loop those two voices through a speaker and sing over to make three,
And keep going until I found my perfect chorus
And then I'd pick a new song and do it again
Because I loved the sound of all of me together
– All of you is welcome in the earth realm

In all of my fiction books,
Yes the ones filled with stories,
There is always a scene
And I don't plan this
And maybe it won't happen in the future
But so far
There is always a story
Where the flowers sing
And the trees join in
And then so too do the characters
And whilst yes it may be a little bit embellished
To me this isn't fiction
To me this is life
And the storytelling is an invitation to notice a little bit more magic
And the magic is natural
It's right there singing to us
Underneath our feet
Right before our eyes
Blooming every spring
Without disappearing for the winter
For there is a perfect chorus and the song is always going
It might sound different
But it never ends
– Earth flowers sing to you

EARTH ROOTS SING

Your house has a song
And you can listen to it
You can influence the instruments
I like to think of it as flow
As I move from room to room
Is there a natural harmony
Or is the air getting trapped and blocking the vocal cords?
– Earth can be a really simple magic

Your car sings too
And often you only intently listen when she or he or they sing out of tune
But give yourself the gift available
Appreciate it now
– Harmonise every chance on earth

EARTH ROOTS SING

Your teachers could sing
Maybe not literally
But they had a story
A service
A message
A mission
And you were the subject of it
They wanted you to succeed
In their roots, they wanted you to succeed
And if they didn't act like it
You know they weren't in their song
And that has everything to do with them
And nothing to do with you
– Just because they aren't singing doesn't mean they have no song

However you are
Whoever you are
However life is going
Whatever you are doing
Wherever you aim to be
Whatever you believe
Whoever you believe in
You have a song
– Your song isn't conditional, it's inherent

EARTH ROOTS SING

The more you sing your song
The more harmonious you will be with life
And how you start singing your song,
You might ask,
I would suggest
A simple hum
– Start singing by making sound

A hum
Executed well
Will vibrate
A miniature sound bath for your body
For your insides
From your insides
Humming along
Humming in
Bouncing around
Moving the sound up and down
Give it a go
Have a hum right now
Imagine the sound hitting the inside of your lips
It'll tickle when you get it right!
Move your sound up and down
Notice if the tickle disappears
Bring back the tickle
Did you do it?
– If you did, you just exercised your voice, if you didn't, you just missed the point

Singing isn't about the sound
Not unless you're a singer
But even so
It's about the feeling
It's a movement
It's a letting go
It's a letting be
It's a release
It's a healing
It's a greeting
It's a farewell
It's a raw introduction
It's a real meeting
It's a message
It's a moment in time
It's a mission
It's whatever you want it to be
– You are so much more than a songbird and you are a perfect songbird

In winter
There is a song in you
In summer
There is a song in you
In spring
There is a song in you
In autumn
There is a song in you
It's okay
That your song changes
Your challenge
Is to keep singing it
– Earth roots sing

EARTH ROOTS SING

A song transports you to
A different place
A different time
A different personality
Are you telling me that isn't magic?
– Earth roots sing to cast spells

ELLIE ANN DEIGHTON

Earth comes together
Herbs into a tea
Vegetables into a pot
Big or small
Here to dance into your body
All singing different songs
And if you are listening
You can tell the songs that are meant for you
– Earth roots call

I have certain medicines
Echinacea
Lavender
Cacao
Calendula
Rose
Lion's Mane
Golden Halo
Passionflower
And they sing to me
I have considered writing down their songs
Recording them to be enjoyed by others
And who knows
Maybe there's an album one day coming
'Flowers Calling'
'Plant Allies Calling'
'Earth Allies Calling'
But for now what I have noticed
Is when I meet a plant
If I listen to the song
I will know if it wants to sing in my body
On my body
Near my body
Or away from my body
And I listen to the song
And I have never had a negative time
And if I had to guess, I would say this is why
And I wouldn't be guessing

ELLIE ANN DEIGHTON

For I know the song
– Earth's songs guide

La la la
Give it a go!
– You can't get singing wrong

Even the wind blowing through the leaves of the trees in your local park is a song
What makes you think you don't have one too?
What makes you think your pain couldn't wail into the most beautiful sound?
What makes you think your joy couldn't create the most eloquent laughter?
What makes you think any form of feeling could create a song out of tune?
What's a song in tune anyway?
I send songs to my producer cold turkey
I rawdog into my voice notes on my phone and send them to him
He responds,
"You are in tune with yourself and it's harmonising and it's beautiful. Now can you whip out a piano and get in tune with that so I can craft the music?"
And that's it.
I can sing in tune with myself or with the stars or with the skies or with a harp
Who says one is better than the other?
Perhaps the different tunes have a different purpose?
Perhaps there's no right or wrong, there's just songs and sound and preference?
Perhaps singing out of tune with the piano and in tune with myself, living on the edge of life between keys is better than silence?
– Singing on the earth is better than no singing on the earth

EARTH ROOTS SING

I wouldn't have it any other way
I could only sing
And it's because singing also happens to be my song
But there is power in the voice
And even if singing isn't your superpower
Even if singing isn't part of your mission
I sang at a funeral
I'd sing at a wedding
I love to sing in special moments for people
Singing is on my path
But even if singing is not on yours
It can be a bridge to get you there
There's a reason
That in the seven elements of fulfilment
The earth one is all about singing!
Because when you find your voice
You find yourself
You find your people
You find your life
You find your mission
You find your wholeness
You find your truth
You find your healing
You find your happiness
You find your emotions
You find your alchemy
You find your community
You find your anything

And in the silence after the song
Everything else dissolves
– Singing isn't the path for everyone, but it is a bridge for all

What do I mean when I say singing isn't the path for everyone but it is a bridge for all? Well that's a great question. What I mean is this: You will find your path quicker if you know your voice, if you know how to shift the energy in your body, if you can harmonise with a room, if you can sing alone and with accompaniment.

When you find your voice you will find your power. When you step into the centre of a circle of people singing and you let your voice rip you will come home to yourself. When you come home to yourself? Well that is where life truly begins. Your life. The life where you choose to be the real you. Yes, singing really does do that.
– As with singing, so with life

When you find the power in your voice
When you find your sound
You will realise you can stand out in a crowd
You will realise the very special way that you are different
You will see the way all the other people are different too
And you will stick to your song because you will want to
Not because your song is better
But because it is the best song for you
I stick to my song not because my song is better
But because it is the best song for me
And that is the point
We get into our songs
And we are set free
– Dance to your song while I dance to mine and we will appreciate each other

EARTH ROOTS SING

When you find your song
And you unleash your voice
You will never see the need to compete ever again
Because you will be the essential you
And you will know that nobody can ever be that
– Have you started singing yet?

If you are afraid to sing,
Hum
If you are afraid to hum,
Listen,
If you are afraid to listen,
You can't be helped!
I'm just kidding...
If you are afraid to listen,
Ask yourself why?
I have always been afraid to listen when I thought I knew I wouldn't like the answer
Like I've been afraid to listen to my muse telling me to write
When I really thought I'd rather take a nap
But guess what?
Then I write
And I am oh so glad
And I will listen again
And there will come a time when I am afraid again
I have been afraid to sing
And I will be afraid again
With or without an audience
I have been afraid of being judged
I have been afraid of hurting my voice
I used to scream and scream and scream at the adventure park so that
I lost my voice
Because I thought it was funny
But really I was afraid of the power of my voice
And some days I still am

EARTH ROOTS SING

Some days I am convinced I cannot write
Some days I am confused that people want to listen to my songs
Some days I am ashamed of having ever recorded my voice
And guess what?
There is no rule that says we cannot be afraid
There is only our choice to take a deep breath and sing
– Earth roots don't have to be brave or fearless, they just get to exist

There's a really fun discovery awaiting you
On the other side of finding your voice
I don't know what it is for you
But I know there is one for everyone
Mine was realising I can shine
Being okay with being a bringer of beauty
Learning I can ask for help
Naming what I truly desire
Going for the truth
Stepping into my power
Owning my vision for my body
Being healthier
Feeling more effortless
Ease in honesty
Saying 'I don't know' and meaning it, without making it mean anything
Being kinder and more patient with others
Landing in myself
Being present in my body and my relationships
Leaning into intimacy
Feeling afraid and doing cool things anyway
Loving who I am and all my gifts and talents
Sharing my gifts and talents
Accepting and outsourcing my anti-gifts and anti-talents
Laughing with lightness at my mistakes
Not knowing and having a go anyway
Really, on the other side of finding my voice
Was a big pink permission slip that invisibly wrapped itself around me

EARTH ROOTS SING

And told me to be free
There was an unshackling of my wild
A lot more orgasms
And a heck of a lot more wonderful living
– Find your voice, find your life

I understand
We are all told
That we can or can't sing
And some of us are lied to
And some of us are told the truth
But let me redefine reality with you:
We are all singers
We are all filled with songs
We are not all taught to sing those songs
But we are all equipped with the instruments
So if you sing
Or if you want to sing and think you can't
Know there are a trillion songs within you
There is no one on earth who knows them all
You can sing your way back into connection
Even if you are tone deaf (hola, Grandma!)
Even if you are deaf (hola, Beethoven!)
Even if you a musician
Your voice can always change
You can always be heard differently
Your sound can transform
You can sing
– We are all of the earth and we all have roots and we can all sing

Your Everlasting Symphony
The Epilogue

ELLIE ANN DEIGHTON

Many years after you have gone
Your songs will still be left
The books you wrote, the letters you typed,
The treasures in your chest
The children you had, the others you taught
The people you loved, heart and mind
An everlasting symphony
Cast across space and time
– You are of the earth forever

Your legacy outlives you

Thank you for reading The Elemental Collection

ELLIE ANN DEIGHTON

'It' is GOLD
out now

A thread of GOLD

Gold plays
Like an undertone
To everything we are about
And we can pretend
We don't know it's there
Gold need not scream and shout
It's obvious and healing
It's present and true
It rises to the service
It's in me and you
And whether you like it
Or whether you see
Others will notice it
Your gold is like a dream
It's easy to become
So natural of a talent
You'll notice you are one
With all this hidden talent

ELLIE ANN DEIGHTON

It's hidden to yourself
For it's so plain to you
But others are enamoured
And all you have to do
Is notice you are gold
And let yourself now have it
And see the gold in others
To connect, again enamoured
The gold in you will rise
The more you're looking for it
So dream of your gold tonight
And let your 'it' come forward
– 'It' is GOLD
Not all gold is hard to find
Gold is here. Will you receive it?
Read ***'It' is GOLD*** Now

About the author

She teaches humans how to live in the light of their true selves and she goes first.
Like an integrity radar
Through life
Hers and yours
She will find the cracks
And spit them out
Until your world tastes like honey together
For she is not here to walk alone
And neither are you.
It is no mistake that you are here reading this.
Is it stories in her books calling you in for a journey?
Is her music singing you home to the temple of you?
Is her curriculum asking you to become more of yourself?
Is now the time?
I believe so.
The scientist in her has a hypothesis,
That you are magic,
The facilitator in her
Can prove it,

The witch in her

Can give you the tools to cast it,

The woman in her

Can celebrate you as you shine,

The artist in her

Is on stage creating beside you.

You are magic,

And here,

You will find that you are home.

– about Ellie, author of **Earth Roots Sing**

Author's note

You will never be alone
For you will always have your voice
And roots will always be inside you
Beckoning the return of your feet to the earth
You can close your eyes and see the stones
And you can open your eyes and look for the trees
And you can place your hands on your body and feel the flesh
And you can move your body and hear the earth sing
And even on the darkest days
There can be a light
Because of your willingness to be with your roots and belong to the earth
And the greatest gift you could ever give yourself
Is to learn to
See
Listen
Feel
Receive
Remember
Play

Speak

Be

Earth

And let the real voice inside you ground you into the wild
– Earth is what I teach

And I can teach you to be one with your earth too
Or you can receive my wild voice to your inbox
Subscribe for bonuses at elliedeighton.com/earth

Permission To Pivot
An Invitation

You have a mission here on earth
A unique voice that's yours to birth
A way of being that sees you thrive
A way of living that fills you with life
And what happens though, is overwhelm
So much to do, so many places to go
And so I will ask you
How do you know
When to do what
And when to let go?
When to lean in
And when to say no?
When to go hard
And when to go home?
Well, if you asked, I would tell you
Plain as can be
Permission to Pivot is how
It's structural you see
Because whether you are living your purpose or not
You absolutely have it

And whether you are living in flow or not
Is just a result of your habits
So at P2P - for short, what I call it
I share all my life hacks, so you can recall it
And before you know it
Overwhelming clouds have cleared
Priorities are taken care of
And the stress of life has left the field
So come to this workshop
Live and done-with-you every quarter
And don't wait, enrol now
Live your mission, raise your voice, live life how you want it
– **Permission To Pivot** is the earth-led path

See you there, my friend.
Let's create your Mission Action Plan (your personal MAP)
So your earthly magic sees the earth,
Ellie

Use the discount code EARTHROOTSSING to begin your journey today.
https://www.thegeniusportal.com.au/p2p

Acknowledgements

Clare
Mem
Daphne
Anthony
Peggy
Dock
Paige
Chris
Elissa
Simon
Joseph
Leah
Kel
Guy
Clem
Lachlan
Ann
Tony
Donelle
Robert

Faith

Devin

Lydia

Romina

Gina

Theresa

Anna

Ryan

Cara

Treena

Greg

Craig

Darren

Melissa

Lachie

Aurora

– Thank you for being in the chorus with me, **Earth Roots Sing** wouldn't exist without you.

www.ingramcontent.com/pod-product-compliance
Lightning Source LLC
Chambersburg PA
CBHW071244070526
44583CB00017B/2323